AUALA

Attitude
Unique skills
Achievement
Leadership
Accomplishment

My Transformational Story
from Samoa to New Zealand

Dear Katie,
Your dreams
are within your
reach. Keep
reaching for your
star. Love –
Sieni Richardson
12/7/2024

Sieni Skelton-Richardson

ISBN: 978-0-473-49607-4

Printed and bound by:
PublishMe, New Plymouth, New Zealand
www.publishme.co.nz

Contents

INTRODUCTION

I wrote this book to empower and support any woman who is adventurous, driven, open, and ready to begin her journey to an abundant, fulfilling, purpose-driven life.

I hope to be an inspiration to women who want to make big changes in their lives but are held back by fear.

I hope this book will speak to each woman directly, regardless of who they are and where they are in their life journeys.

It is my intention that my Auala (my road traveled) will be another woman's pathway, and that, in turn, each woman I help will share her same journey with others so they, too, can have success in their own journeys. Since my two trips to Samoa, both in 2017, for my sister's funeral and again in 2018 for her unveiling, I was amazed at the flock of people turning up to show their respect. She has impacted many people in her own unselfish ways. She was an entrepreneur with a generous heart. People not only showed up to donate their time, food, and rental equipment, but they also donated financially. It was overwhelming. I was really touched, inspired, and I wanted to give back and make an impact on others the way she had while she was alive.

The idea of this book kind of grew from there, and it has been boiling for some time. I started thinking about my life, and where I am today, and where I would like to be in the future. The concept of Auala came to light when I thought of how relevant it is for me, especially being a Samoa woman, to pave the way for others.

Auala is the Samoa word for road. I have used this as a metaphor: A—Attitude, U—Unique skills, A—Accomplishment, L—Leadership, A—Achievement. My journey to where I am today is comprised of these five letters in the word Auala. Throughout this book, I will walk you through my Auala, how it all started, and what prompted the thought to take my journey. With any road, you will always come across potholes, uphills, downhills, smooth and straight road, roundabouts, curves, and corners. So it is never a smooth-sailing trip when you embark on any journey, but these things, to me, are blocks or pieces of our own jigsaw puzzles. We have to piece them together ourselves. The blocks are highs, lows, challenges, opportunities, and successes we will encounter along the way. How we respond defines us.

Mark 10:42–45: "For even the Son of Man did not come to be served, but to serve."

"A woman is like a tea bag—you never know how strong she is until she gets in hot water."

Eleanor Roosevelt

ASPECTS OF AUALA INFLUENCING SUCCESS OF THE LIFE JOURNEY!

It is believed that there are various ways to achieve goals and that everyone is able to accomplish greater things in life, whether it be short-term or long-term goals. However, it is significant to understand and discover what it takes to reach such a level where life is prosperous and to accept the notion that people have different methods of reaching a successful milestone in life. Moreover, there are many contributing factors to ensuring a successful journey to achieving a dream or goal.

One of those factors is Auala, or pathway/road traveled. The Samoan term, auala, can be expressed and defined in many contexts, depending on what is relative to the subject. For example, Auala can be used in the Samoa culture when someone goes to meet another family for the first time.

In this case, you would often hear the older people in the family ask the question, "O le a lou auala mai?" (What is the purpose of your journey?)

I have been navigating through pathways to reach my dreams and goals with the intention to share my Auala with others as an empowerment to them. It is my hope that others will be able to learn from my story and benefit from my knowledge.

There is a saying, "Perfect trees do not exist." This quote serves to describe my Auala to the kind of life I have now. During my journey, I testify that I have gone through good times and encountered difficult obstacles. As quoted above, perfect trees do not exist because trees need water and sunlight in order to prosperously grow. Similarly, I made hard decisions, mistakes, and fought my winning battles to get to where I am today. Metaphorically, on the road, you have a choice as to whether you want to be the driver or the passenger. At this stage of my life, I want to be the driver, steering my own wheel in the direction I want. People travel every day through different pathways on the road. I notice this daily when I am behind the steering wheel. It's fascinating to see the flow of cars in different directions. This reminds me of how not to be swayed to the wrong side of the Auala, or make a wrong turn, and instead use Auala to help steer you to take the necessary steps in the right direction in your life journey.

All these complications I have encountered throughout my life directed me to the area of improvement and helped me later become successful in life. As an old saying goes, "We all make mistakes, but the best thing about making mistakes is that we learn from them."

Through my Auala, you will learn to take the right steps and avoid repeating mistakes. As a Samoan proverbial phrase states: "Ia seu le manu ma taga'i i le galu." (Catch the sea bird and watch out for the wave.) Choose the right Auala, as it is the only way to ensure your arrival to the right destination.

MY STORY

I was born in the village of Malie in Samoa and grew up in American Samoa. Currently, I make my home in New Zealand. I am the daughter of loving parents, who are both deceased, and the youngest of seven children: two boys and five girls. I am a sister, wife, mother, and aunt. I was born Catholic and remain a strong practicing Catholic to this day.

I remember lots of family members were always around at home, especially my ever-present grandparents. My grandparents were very nurturing and spoiled my siblings and me. This tradition of giving love was passed down from them to my father and from my father to my siblings and me.

I attended Malie Primary School until my father sent me to a Catholic girls' school called St. Mary's Primary School Savalalo, where I started at standard two (year five in today's school-year system). My father had the best intentions for his children's future, so it was imperative for him to give us good opportunities. He highly valued good education and believed the cost of private schools for us was worth it.

I lived in Samoa (at the time, it was known as Western Samoa) until the age of twelve, when my dad and step-mother uplifted the family to American Samoa in 1982. They enrolled me at another Catholic school called St. Francis School from year six to year eight, after which I went on to Faasao High School, a girls-only Catholic high school.

From my graduation in 1989, I lived and worked in American Samoa until 1999 when I emigrated to New Zealand in search of better opportunities and to further my education. My father's initial intention was to migrate with his family to New Zealand for a better future, but it was a lot of money, hassle, and stress to make the move with seven children. I felt so grateful that my journey was leading me to the place he had initially set his sights on.

When we were living in Western Samoa, my father was the breadwinner of the family. He made all the decisions, and I looked up to him for many years of my life. He was a very determined and hard-working person. He worked in American Samoa and would fly home for the weekend. On occasions he couldn't travel, he would send money over.

My mother would have to borrow money from other family members and friends to last us a few days before my father's paycheck turned up. We often had to forgo some pleasures and make the money stretch to cover the essentials. On days we had no coffee or tea, we resorted to drinking lemon leaves (moegalo in Samoa). The taste was not my favorite, but it was what was available to us in the meantime.

It amazes me how tough things must have been for my parents having to raise seven kids on one person's income. I take my hat off to my father, because he made it work. Providing shelter and security for his family was his number-one priority. Thanks to my father, we had a secure, safe home with food on the table and good education. I am forever grateful to my dad for giving my siblings and me a solid foundation.

These early lessons passed down from my parents have been embedded in me, and I will continue to treasure what I have learned throughout my whole life's journey.

"A" Represents Attitude, and Why Does Attitude Matter?

A—Attitude: For me, the first letter of the word Auala represents attitude. Most people define attitude as the way humans behave. Moreover, some may interpret attitude based on how we think, feel, and act. Therefore, we must define attitude in order to understand its importance and value, especially its positive and negative impacts on our life journeys. Attitude is a settled way of thinking or feeling about something or someone, typically reflected in a person's behavior. Given that attitude serves as a reflection of our personalities and who we are, this is everything; it is within me and all of us. It shows up in everything we do and don't do.

It was really up to me to take full responsibility of the

path I was destined to have while I was living on the island. I believe it was having the right attitude that propelled me to explore this side of the world, where I am today. I could have easily done the opposite and stayed with the status quo. But somehow, somewhere, an inner voice pushed through and kept persuading me to challenge my status quo and see where it would lead me.

Reflectively, the question is, does attitude matter? Does it impact our life journeys? Well, of course, having the right attitude is essential, as it is a reflection of our personal values and who we are as people. Attitude matters because it determines the way we think, act, and respond to external and internal circumstances. On the other hand, attitude has a huge impact on our lifelong journeys. The decisions we make derive from our attitude. Therefore, the attitude we express toward our decisions in life determines our destination. As coined by Maya Angelou:

"If you don't like something, change it. If you can't change it, change your attitude."

With that in mind, when we have the right attitude, we are able to see situations, problems, solutions, and processes from different angles. And believing in ourselves allows us to make connections with the right people in order to leverage new resources or move in new directions. While it can also be alienating when you are so driven to gain a greater advantage—at these times, we pull back and isolate ourselves from others—there is a reason why we do it. We just need to make sure things are actually done. Although some people could perceive it as compulsive and antisocial, people with such drive direct this attribute toward very clear results and achieve great outcomes.

Thus, in this book, I will touch on how each letter of the word Auala highlights and tells the story of the journey. I totally believe, as I progress through my Auala, I will encounter new things which could potentially stir some interests, and, knowing who I am, with the right attitude of continuously learning, I will explore them in this lifetime.

When I think back and visualize myself standing on the edge of the Auala debating internally what action to take, I remember that that defined moment was the biggest determinant of the life I would have. Had I not taken that one step forward on the Auala, I would have never seen what this side of the Auala had to offer. Attitude brought me here and will also take me to other places, depending on where I want to go. Everything in this book portrays the strong sense of attitude. Every day, I am faced with choices, and I am the only person who can give myself the best possible answer.

It also helps when you have been taught to have good values to live by every day.

The Power of Visualization

A lot of people have been writing and talking about the power of visualization. I am a true believer in this teaching. I had visualized myself moving to New Zealand and achieving my goals which I set before I set sail on this journey.

Nelson Mandela has written extensively on how visualization helped him maintain a positive attitude while being imprisoned for twenty-seven years. "I thought continually of the day when I would walk free. I fantasized about what I would like to do," he wrote in his autobiography. Visualization works well to improve attitude.

You can have the right attitude, but if you fail to act on the things you want to change in your life, your chances of achieving success in life will only be limited to your imagination.

My Life on the Island

My siblings and I were brought up in a devout Catholic family. My parents—especially my father—were very tough and strict with us kids, but there was no denying their love for us. My father always had the intention to be a good provider for his family. He wanted to make sure that we would have a good upbringing at home and outside of home in a good school environment.

I was very fortunate to graduate from high school thanks to my parents' support. The dream of most high school graduates at the time was to go to a university for higher education and qualifications. It was definitely a dream of mine as well back then, but unfortunately, my grades weren't good enough to land a scholarship. Money was tight, so I changed my direction toward finding a job.

In Western Samoa, our house sat right next to our church. The only religion I knew growing up was Catholicism. Sunday mass and school were a traditional routine for me and my siblings growing up, so there was no excuse for us not to get involved. My parents made sure we went to church.

Having those structured routines built up over time helped with my personal growth.

Even today, I carry this Sunday tradition of going to church. The teachings of the church plus values learned from my parents helped shape me and keep me grounded today. The values of family, love, respect, and how we treat others as we wanted to be treated permeates through my life. It was that attitude that helped me sit through my high school years and complete whatever was necessary to graduate.

I was not happy when I couldn't go to college due to our financial constraints at the time, but I had to adjust my way of thinking to be respectful and accepting of the choice my parents had to make. Certainly, if money wasn't an issue, there wouldn't have been any hesitation in supporting me in my aspirations.

Change in Direction

For ten years after I left high school, I worked at the StarKist Samoa Inc. tuna cannery in Pago Pago, American Samoa. My first job was a fish cleaner, a low-level entry job which didn't require a diploma.

The cannery was a smelly factory, but to those who worked there, it only smelled of money. It is money that puts food on the table and creates livelihood for many people on the island. It would have been some time before I could start earning, because there were lots of other graduates looking for jobs at the same time and, being a small island, jobs can be hard to find for a non-experienced graduate like myself. I was happy when I started earning money, even though it was a small amount. I would rather have smelly work than beg for money.

Thinking back, I feel grateful that I took the path into employment first rather than carrying on with education. Fresh from high school, I didn't know what I wanted to do for my career, so going to college would have been a waste of my time and what little money we had. I didn't wait for the right job before I submitted my application. I knew I had to start from somewhere. I was looking for different jobs but hadn't been successful. I landed the fish-cleaner job quickly because it didn't require a lot of knowledge. I started earning real money, and I was in my flow.

I was determined not to clean fish for long, and that determination pushed me to often apply for various jobs when they came up in other departments within the organization. I progressed to various administration roles. There were lots of jobs I applied for but didn't get. Timing is everything. Some of those job vacancies weren't the right fit for me, but I took failure seriously in those early days.

Often when things don't quite go our way, we have unhealthy internal dialogue, which can demoralize our confidence. I felt unworthy and had very low self-esteem when I wasn't a successful applicant, but, gradually, I learned how to see past those setbacks. I had to learn how to navigate my self-doubt and control my emotions in order to evaluate my actions and reactions. Nothing comes easily, and success doesn't come without a fight.

Doing the same thing over and over makes you feel stagnant. I didn't want to look back in thirty years and have regrets because I didn't change my life, push myself educationally, experience new adventures, or take myself out of my comfort zone. So I decided to search for better opportunities in New Zealand.

Let's not wait for the perfect time, because it might never come. Instead, aim just to do your very best. The real shift is in our approach and our mindset, and this is the shift I believe we, as women, must take if we need a change in our lives.

It takes the right attitude to lead your own life. My determination and eagerness to learn prompted the decisions I made in different situations. There is a widely used phrase in the Bible which serves as a great encouragement to any person seeking answers:

> *"Ask and it will be given to you;*
> *seek and you will find;*
> *knock and the door will be opened to you."*
> *(Matthew 7:7)*

Don't just stop when someone says no. Keep knocking on doors until one opens. My advancement to different jobs was a result of my "I can do it" attitude. As soon as something spiked my interest, I would go for it and push my luck. My decision to change my direction was fueled by my ambition to walk my Auala and make the sacrifices necessary to achieve the life I wanted. Your attitude and ambition will only take you as far as the change you will make in your everyday life.

"U" Represents Unique Skills and Why They Matter

U—Unique Skills: We are all born with our own unique talents, and some of us have had to learn different talents and skills for our own benefits. It is not enough to rely solely on talent. You need to put in hard work as well to reach your dreams. Your can-do attitude simply lifts you to different playing fields, forcing you to play at the level you are meant to play. While any journey can take you to various places and different landscapes, it also takes you deep into self-actualization, to a sense of being fully aware of your true potential.

It is only through my own Auala that I began to learn more about myself and have come to the realization that attitude (A), which I have touched on, combined with a unique set of skills (U), plus other components I will expand upon throughout this book, contribute to the achievement of my desired outcome.

The same goes for anyone who is at a point in their lives where enough is enough. It's time to change your game, take control of your life, and charge ahead. We have to be willing to learn skills and practice them wholeheartedly if we want to change the desired outcome.

Goal Setting

When I was twenty-nine, I made the bold move to leave my family behind in search of better opportunities and to reach new goals in my life.

My dad's expression said it all. He didn't speak to me

for three weeks prior to my departure. He seemed like he would miss the money I was giving him to help run our household more than he would miss me.

I was a strong-headed daughter. All I wanted to do was move to New Zealand and achieve something for myself.

Before I embarked on my journey to New Zealand in late December 1999, I set three big life goals:

1 - Earn a degree

2 - Become a New Zealand citizen

3 - Own my own home

Earn a Degree

I had seen the life an educated person could have and the impact it could have on their families and people around them. I dreamed of that life. Earning a degree would solidify my dream on personal and professional levels.

On the personal level, my degree was proof I should never settle for less, but rather keep challenging myself to achieve more. The experience at an early age when my family moved islands proved to me I could adapt to change and new environments.

On the professional level, of course, my earning potential was higher with a degree. A degree represented power, strength, determination, hard work, attitude, confidence, and discipline.

The experience was challenging in so many ways. I had a big break from studies after I finished high school, and coming back to school had its own challenges—such as the language. I could speak English, but I didn't feel confident with it, so practicing reading, speaking, writing, and presenting in English was my top priority. I had to raise my game and put in many, many hours of dedication and self-discipline. I needed to set my own rules and routines.

I reached my first goal on May 7, 2003, when I was awarded a Bachelor of Commerce degree from the University of Auckland. Hearing my name called out at the graduation ceremony was my proudest moment thus far. It was such a great feeling, and the sense of achievement was made even more special by having my brother and his family, my friends, and partner Daryl (now my husband) present. I also knew for sure my parents and other members of my family in Samoa and other parts of the world had cheered me on and shared this great joy. My success was their success.

I was the first in my family to attend university, and today many of my family members have been inspired to follow in my footsteps.

Becoming a New Zealand Citizen

I was a citizen of Western Samoa, but a permanent resident of American Samoa. To enter New Zealand for my studies, I had to apply for a student visa. I was granted a two-year visa to study, because I had applied for entry to the two-year diploma in the business course. I then continued on to my degree, which was another two years of studies.

I was an international student, so the tuition fees were very expensive compared to students born in New Zealand. This was a motivating factor for me to do well and to complete my studies hastily. It pushed me to explore and ask questions on how I could become a resident.

After many visits to the immigration office and a lot of waiting, I finally had my chance to meet with an immigration officer. Thankfully, I gathered all the documents required, and I became a permanent resident in the year 2000. The transition from resident to citizenship status was easier. I became an official New Zealand citizen on September 17, 2002, and my second goal was achieved.

At first, I had conflicting feelings about becoming a citizen. I worried about losing my identity as a Samoan woman. But I've learned that people make sacrifices for good reasons. For me, there were benefits from the transition in terms of my education. It was such a relief to know I didn't have to pay the international tuition fees and could qualify for a student loan to further my education.

It was a painful process to go through because of the amount of paperwork, but the process is there for a reason. My persistence paid off when I became a citizen. I now have the ability to travel in and out of New Zealand with less hassle. Another advantage was being able to help family members visit New Zealand.

Opportunities here are endless, but it comes down to

the individual and how they make a life for themselves.

Owning my Own Home

After a year living with my brother and his family, I made a decision to go flatting somewhere closer to the city and my university. I found a one-bedroom apartment downtown which was only a ten-minute walk to university. I wouldn't say it was a flashy accommodation, but it was a starting point of my flatting journey. I stayed there for six months, then moved to a different flat when my friend from university mentioned she was looking for a roommate. My ten-minute walk became a twenty-five-minute walk, but I didn't mind it at all because I really enjoyed living in that big seven-bedroom house.

The house was filled with scholarship medical students from Malaysia and Singapore, so I was the odd one out— but, thanks to my friend's recommendation, they accepted me, so long as I was happy to comply by their house rules. Well, the house met my three criteria of price, location, and people, so everything else was secondary.

My third ambitious goal was to own my own home, because I believed it would give me that sense of belonging and security. Fortunately, I had some money locked away for when I needed it. That time came after my meeting with a bank advisor one day, and she suggested I put my money to work through investing in property. She booked me an appointment with their mobile mortgage broker the very next day. He was helpful and smart, with lots of valuable knowledge—and, to top it off, he was a property investor himself. I was the lucky one at the other end of the conversation, receiving all his knowledge as he happily shared with me.

That meeting changed my life. It opened my eyes to possibilities I never knew existed, and from that one action of signing my name on the dotted line, I was the proud owner of my first investment on June 6, 2003. Not so bad for someone who arrived in New Zealand in late 1999. My third goal was achieved, and with it, the proof that I could confidently decide and design how I wanted my life to be.

I am thankful they placed that mortgage broker into my path because he flexed my thinking from home ownership to property investing. More doors opened up with opportunities that led me to eventually start my own residential property business on the side.

When I retrace my journey of how I achieved these three goals, I attribute my success to the combination of these distinctive characteristics:

Step 1. Clarity: I was clear about my goals.

Step 2. Persistence: I was hungry and didn't give up.

Step 3. Focus: I stayed on the roadmap until I achieved it.

Step 4. Action: I took action. My goals wouldn't have been achieved if I didn't take action.

There is always a process. Through this process, I learned

that having belief in myself reassured me that I can do great things. There was something special in me, a burning desire to succeed, that made it possible to achieve those goals.

It taught me that I should never limit myself in thinking I'm only an island girl. Initially, I had self-doubts, but I believe my spiritual self also played an important part in my journey. I have rediscovered the real me.

My father was so happy and proud when I phoned to tell him about it. I got excited and wanted to keep the momentum going, so I set a new goal: to buy one property a year to reach ten properties by the year 2013.

I bought my second property in 2004, but then things took a turn when I met my husband in 2004. I moved to his hometown in July 2005, and we got married that December. A different set of happy events diverted my attention from my property goal.

Soon after my wedding, I received some sad news that Mum had been admitted to the hospital. I flew over as soon as I could, but when I arrived in Samoa, she was already unconscious. Mum died on December 21, 2005. I never had the opportunity to say goodbye.

We have to learn to live through life's challenges. Learning to be strong mentally was, and is, super important to me.

In 2006, just when I thought I was coming right again, dreaded news from home came that Dad was unwell. I flew home again to be by my dad's side.

Lucky for me, Dad was still conscious and able to have a conversation when I got there. The last week with my dad was a precious, treasured moment. I didn't have that time with my mother, but having that time with my father got me mentally ready for what was to come. I had to go back to New Zealand, and said my final goodbyes. I soon received a phone call that he had passed away. It shattered me, even though I thought I was mentally prepared. I think the realization that the physical bond was gone forever and that he wouldn't be there again was the hardest to accept.

I view funerals not as a sad thing but a celebration with all the people Dad had touched in life. For us, it was to celebrate his legacy. It was also a reminder for us to leave the same legacy when that time comes.

Lesson learned: Live now, live fully, and spread love and peace to everyone you come across every day.

The more I understood the validity of goal setting in my life, the more I value this unique skill because it paved my Auala to the successes I have had, and I will keep using it and keep at it for future ambitions of mine. There is a strong correlation between goal setting and self-confidence, and the more confidence you build up, the more certain you are to achieve your goals. You will gain skills that will help you design and execute your own plan to suit you, how to deal with setbacks, and to be able to fend off the temptations and pressures that will get in your way.

RITUALS AND HABITS

Form Good Habits for Success

Ritual: a series of actions or type of behavior regularly and invariably followed by someone.

There is a repetitive message from successful people: form good habits. We all have good and bad habits, but it is our utmost task to work on those bad habits that hold us back from realizing our potential, who we really are, and what we can achieve.

I have a daily morning ritual. I normally get up at 4:30 a.m., no matter what time I had gone to bed (as long as I have had no less than six hours of decent, uninterrupted sleep). I pray for twenty-five minutes, followed by twenty minutes of cardio exercise on the bike while listening to or reading a motivational book, then ten minutes of weights.

These habits didn't just happen overnight. I have been

doing this for over twenty years now, and I have to admit, I definitely feel good about myself every time I do it. If I miss a day, I feel guilty that I am not prioritizing myself.

When my day starts with my daily ritual, I know the rest of my day will be good. Exercise and positive thoughts first thing in the morning creates a breakthrough on my outlook.

The two habits I now concentrate on building are my financial habits and health habits.

Why Financial Habits?

I feel it's critical for me to focus on my financial habits because I believe if this area of my life gets attention, then I will live a less anxious life. I can remember the struggle of living paycheck to paycheck, seeing the money disappear fast. Money-smart people would have said my priorities weren't in the right place, and now I would totally agree with them.

There is so much danger in not knowing the truth about finances. I had to learn to be more aware of my spending habits. I had to repeatedly ask myself, am I buying something because of a need or because of a want? Being able to differentiate between these two enables me to better manage the inflow and outflow of my money. It helps me to make informed decisions and enjoy investing in properties, shares, and courses to help with self-development, family holidays, birthday parties, charities, and so forth. Today, I recognize the difference in my well-being. I feel having control of my money helps me feel calm; my mind is freer and more relaxed, but it is still a work in progress.

Everything is a process, and I need to enjoy the journey along the way.

Obviously, we find it difficult when we have to change habits we've built up over time. We all know and understand that change takes a long time, and it requires repeated experiments and failures. And when we know and understand how a habit operates, we can identify triggers that form habits and gain control over them.

When I started getting serious about creating good financial habits, the first thing I needed to focus on was my mindset about money. I needed to have a healthy relationship with money. I often hear stories of people winning the lottery who then lost it all within a few years. We need to be mindful of our actions and behaviors when large sums of money come our way. I believe if we can learn to manage small amounts of money well, we should be able to manage substantial amounts if we are lucky enough to land big wins.

Because I had envisioned that I would like to live and have a good life and help others, I was willing to do whatever it took to turn that vision into reality.

True financial literacy gave me the confidence to pursue my dream of owning my first house. Back in 2003, the loan amount of $155,000 was massive. To some people, it would have been scary, but to me, it wasn't. I understood early on the difference between a bad debt and good debt. That debt was definitely a good debt, because I had bought an income-producing asset with it, which still to this day gives me passive income. This asset helped grow my property portfolio exponentially.

Often, we are told that education is the key to success and that we have to practice certain behaviors, such as positive rituals and routines, to reach success. Unfortunately, we often fail to examine what it takes to become a successful person. As a result of this failure, we must question what is in education that you can use as a key to succeed in life. It is clear that most people can go to college and graduate with a degree; however, only a few college graduates come out successful. As coined by a Samoan proverbial phrase, "E tele ē tausiniō, ae to'aitiiti ē filifilia." (Many can compete, but only a few will win.)

I firmly believe the key to becoming successful is practicing acquired knowledge from school to solve and determine the results of real-life situations. Through this process, you apply your educational knowledge to overcome obstacles in life and positively gain unique skills depending on the situation. In fact, having unique skills and applying my educational knowledge to find a better and healthier lifestyle allowed me to succeed in life. I have read lots of articles about so many amazing women and men who were not necessarily smarter, luckier, or better than I am. The main difference between me and those people was that they've acquired certain skills, knowledge, and experience which made them powerful. Plus, they were remarkably undaunted by unkindness and negativities they came across through their life journeys because they knew they were destined for greatness, and they took themselves seriously.

I had to take myself seriously if I was to achieve my goals. My plan was to continue walking my Auala with laser focus to reach my desired destination. Because there were steps I had to take to get there, acquiring the right skills was important to me. It takes courage to walk on the straight lanes and follow my own road. There were times I would get out of bed and didn't want to do my morning rituals. I relate this scenario to coming to a steep hill on a particular part of the road, then you stop, and tell yourself it's too hard, therefore debating with yourself whether to forge ahead or turn back.

I knew how I would feel if I didn't do them. It is the same feeling when you plan to meet with a friend at a certain time and place and you don't show up or make contact with her about your reason for being a no-show. You let that person down. That is how I feel when I let myself down.

Unfortunately, when we make a bold statement and step into our genius, resistance is intent on keeping us small—but we rely on our inner strength to act and to do things despite difficulties, and we persevere. This is you taking control of your steering wheel.

Personal Experiences and Breakthrough

Sports were a big part of my life back on the island. I actively participated in soccer, netball, and running. I was fortunate enough to make it into the representative teams in American Samoa in the above sports, partaking in inter-island South Pacific competitions and Oceania track and field meets. That was probably where I got my competitive edge, always striving for excellence.

Although my teams may not have won medals in all

those competitions, they taught me how to be a good team player. When competing in a solo sport, you alone have to play your own game, fight your own battle, and win or lose from your own effort, not anyone else's. Self-motivation and discipline is important in the solo environment, whereas in a team environment, you must work together to achieve that end goal. I also learned skills of listening, communication, respect, reliability, and how to be a good loser.

Additionally, I learned how to accept that we were sometimes not strong enough to beat other teams, but as long as we gave our best, that was all we could do. We would analyze where we had gone wrong and how to avoid making the same mistake again. This is the review process I go through with most of the decisions I make today, whether they be at home, work, or elsewhere. If I don't, recurring mistakes will derail me from my road to success.

Beyond sports, I also competed in beauty pageants in American Samoa. My first attempt landed me the Second Runner-Up position. The following year, I placed First Runner-Up. I was closer because each time I kept working on things that didn't work the previous year. I was resilient, and my confidence had taken a turn for the better. The following year, they crowned me Miss American Samoa 1998 to 1999. I felt very honored and grateful to God and the people who have supported me in my journey.

I was surrounded by very supportive women, and from then on, I could see the value each woman could add to another woman's confidence and self-esteem. The encouragement and inspirational backing from those women had made my role easier and less stressful. With the support of these women, I was walking on a less-daunting path; it didn't seem foreign because they held my hand and guided me every step of the way in the right direction.

The title came with a lot of benefits: traveling, attending government functions, invitations to school events, judging school beauty pageants, and more. I was a property of that organization, but I raised my hand to accept the responsibilities and expectations that came with the role. They required a lot of dedication on my part to show up, carry the title with pride, represent them at events, and be a role model to other young ladies who also have aspirations to follow my path. Another challenge was having to prioritize my time with pageant events while keeping my job, as that was still my main income supporting me and my family. As with most things in life, there is never a journey without challenges.

Looking back, I am grateful for those challenges because they made me stronger. Thanks to the amazing support from other women, I was able to see things through and tackle each challenge strategically. I would encourage all young ladies to take part in things like this because it is a great way to build your confidence, to represent yourself, and to represent your culture.

You and I have a purpose to show the world that there is beauty, intelligence, and wisdom within Pacific women, and we should carry that with us to whatever corner of the world we make our journey to. Don't let anyone or anything hold you back from achieving the dream you are destined to have.

These life experiences and memories serve as a constant reminder to me of how far I have come—the road I have traveled to get to where I am today. When I have a low moment in my life (which I often do), I reflect back on positive experiences, little wins, and life-enriching encounters I have had with different wonderful people around me, because it helps bring me to my equilibrium stage of happiness.

As Eleanor Roosevelt once said:

"The purpose of life is to live it, to taste experience to the utmost, to reach out eagerly and without fear for newer and richer experience."

Nothing is ever truly perfect, nor entirely a tragedy, but we have to take responsibility and accept the ups and downs of one's life journey and beyond. We should use the skills we've built up over time to transform ourselves into better beings, so we can achieve a meaningful and fulfilling life. I believe we need to truly experience a breakthrough on our outlook on life, whatever good or bad comes out of it. We have to accept that is life, and we should embrace it.

My Auala stemmed from having the right attitude. To be selected was proof of my attitude to our coach that I deserved a spot in the team. The selection was a result of my preparation, discipline, and sacrifice. All that was from improving my attitude and changing my behavior. We all know this is difficult to do, as people must want to change.

In light of this book, our journey in life is to keep sharing our road, our Auala, with others.

WEALTH

Wealth is being able to have control of my life and my time. It means choosing what is best for me and my family, not relying on others to make those choices for me. It means being confident in financial decisions to grow my wealth.

I regularly hear people say, "No health no wealth." To me, that saying is so relevant today. I have seen how left-field events related to people's health have caused sadness, anger, depression, family separation, and so forth. It's a sad reality, because a lack of wealth is something that we can control and change ourselves. If we reach out to the right people, they will be more than willing to lend us a hand.

My learnings on wealth creation started when I was introduced to property investing. Attending seminars and speaking with people with the same interests helped me gain a deeper understanding of the concept.

Money Relationships

Don't be a slave to money, but know how to make it work for you. I have seen what money provides for my family and my church. One of the most joyful memories I have of money was when my sister, who had breast cancer, came over to New Zealand for her operation. She was not a citizen, so anything to do with her health would cost twice as much or more than what I would pay. It set me back $40,000, but I have no regrets. She needed help, and what is the use of money when you don't have *love*?

When you know your contribution has made a difference to someone else's life, you feel good about it and see life differently.

I have learned how to set a budget with an Excel spread-sheet. It is easy to do, but the hardest part is getting started. An alternative is the use of your mobile phone. I have found that my Excel spreadsheet works well for me because it records all monthly expenses. This is very helpful because I can proactively look ahead at what expenses or bills are coming up. I can then make sure I have enough funds available to allocate and that can be transferred on time to the correct accounts for payments.

Have an Emergency Fund

If your car breaks down today, will you have the excess money to pay for the repairs? If you need to go to your doctor tomorrow, could you afford to pay for the visit and the medication? If you get sick suddenly and cannot work for months, how would you handle that situation?

When my financial advisor first asked me these questions, I froze. I started to feel a sense of panic because everything she said made so much sense. She recommended I list all the regular expenses I pay every month and see how much it adds up to. That should be the amount in my emergency fund.

I had to adjust some of my behaviours and embrace small changes to get this critical emergency fund put in place. I set aside enough to cover one month's expenses, then two, then three. Over a period of many months, with clear focus and a lot of self-discipline, I have now set aside enough to cover six months of expenses. My goal is to keep saving until I have enough set aside for a full year. I need to persevere and be dedicated to this process. It will not be easy—I can guarantee that—but I know it is not impossible.

Leverage

When I started my property investing journey, "leverage" became a recurring word in my everyday conversations. The successful people I have been following were in a different level of success because they didn't use the money they already had to invest but rather leveraged and used other people's money. They used borrowed money to fund the things they wanted to invest in, and achieved good returns from those investments while working at accelerating their wealth. The principle made sense to me when I was just starting out in property. My small capital coupled with the bank's money and borrowed funds enabled me to accumulate assets. I wouldn't have been able to achieve that if I didn't understand how leverage worked.

Leverage Through Network and Relationships

A great network will work to your advantage. You need to leverage each other's knowledge and expertise. We don't always have all the answers, but people in your network might know someone who does. I have a network of friends and businesswomen, both locally and globally, who I reach out to when I need help. I recommend surrounding yourself with like-minded people, because you can encourage and push each other toward your individual goals.

Leverage Your Time

Using leverage has contributed to the success of many successful people. I prefer the hands-off approach—outsourcing good people because I value my time and I want to leverage it.

The Auala my parents journeyed was tough, but their perseverance to provide a better life for our family surpassed the challenges they faced. We weren't wealthy in the sense of finances, but we were wealthy in terms of having minimal resources or necessities in life. We had shelter, and we were safe. Whatever money we had was just enough to make ends meet for the family. There was a good sense of money management in our household—or, one can say we were able to manage whatever money we had.

Wealth creation is a skill itself. Once I realized that this skill was going to give me more choices in life, I did not hesitate to start on my own Auala and learn all that was necessary to have financial security from here on out. I have witnessed many folks going through stress and pain just to make ends meet. That forced me to continue searching for opportunities and ways to help fine-tune this skillset and create better processes to enable this part of my life to work without much effort. One of the important things I have learned from my many mentors is to actually do the actions early and not keep delaying things.

HEALTH

As a person from a family with several health issues, I know the importance of prioritizing my health. I want to live a longer life and be around for my family, especially with my daughter being an only child.

Mindset is the first thing to focus on. While I can't do much about my genetics, what I can change are things I control myself: the food I eat and keeping active. My decisions and actions dictate my behavior.

Every day, I stick to my routine of twenty minutes of cardio on my bike, followed by ten minutes of weight exercises. I believe in having consistency daily. It's much easier and saves me a lot of time because I have the exercise equipment at home, so I don't have to leave and drive somewhere else to do my exercises. When we have kids and run businesses from home, many of us end up feeling overwhelmed and burned out because we are constantly running everywhere. I purposefully make the decision to invest in these machines for home use because time is valuable, and it's imperative I utilize it wisely at home

Knowing that breast cancer runs in the family, I ensure I have annual breast cancer screenings. In New Zealand, women are entitled to a subsidized mammogram every two years, but I have proactively talked to my doctor to request for this additional service in between the subsidized biannual services. I humbly encourage women to talk to your doctor and get those checks done. Do it for yourself, your children, and your family. Be proactive with your health.

Conscious Eating

At any Samoan family gathering, food is a focal point. We love our traditional food and how it brings families together. We always enjoy a lot of laughter and family conversations around a table full of delicious, colorful food. It is so easy to overindulge at these gatherings, but over time, I have noticed my eating habits have changed tremendously from my usual diet when I was back on the island. The more you gain an understanding of the benefits of certain food, the more you lean toward the path of consuming those types of food. Vegetables and fruits are a must on my grocery list, and I try to ensure vegetables are on the dinner plate every night in our household. Instilling small changes at home is a good example to set for kids.

I control what food I put in my mouth, so I can't blame anyone else for my actions. To shift the blame to others shows I am not being honest with myself, not taking myself seriously, and not valuing my health.

Have Routine Health Checks

I have yearly health checks with my doctor, even when I don't feel pain or aches. The small price to pay for this doctor's visit is worth an early detection of potential health problems. These checks may allow for earlier treatment, resulting in the better outcome we all hope for.

I wish my sister, who had lost her battle with breast cancer, had taken this kind of active approach with her health. She may have had more time with her family. I encourage women to make health a priority, especially for your family and children who are depending on you.

I remember very well our conversation one evening, when my sister's health was deteriorating in the hospital. She had things she hoped to do once she got her health back, but unfortunately she never had that second chance. I still think about it today. It is a reminder for me to get into gear, because I am living on borrowed time.

Health and wealth are interconnected. If your health is in order, your productivity increases, and you have more energy to earn, grow wealth, live, and serve.

There are certain fundamentals we need to follow if we need to achieve good health, and we should endeavor to do those things with intensity and purpose. The results, good or bad, are reflections of my own effort and the kind of attitude I brought to those situations. For instance, I maneuver my car on the road so I maintain my position in my lane, but there are things that will cause distraction, such as phones or keeping the kids calm. As soon as you take your eyes off the road, some potential harm may occur. The same applies to our attitude with our health. This part of our lives is critical to wealth creation.

Furthermore, I notice a weakness in so many women is putting many hours of hard work toward our families and careers while dedicating minimal time to our individual wants and needs. I associate this to our nurturing nature as mothers. We want to ensure our family is well looked after. Often, this lack of attention to ourselves can alter our health and well-being. This is why immersing ourselves in a positive and healthy environment can give us a positive direction to good lifestyle habits.

Attitude is often used to describe a person. How would you like someone to describe you? What kind of attitude do you have?

I have an intense drive to achieve my goal of keeping active through my twenty daily minutes of cardio exercise. I believe if I bring a good attitude I can maintain my health and well-being. My family is well aware of the emphasis I put into my health, my scheduled workouts at home, meal preparation, having enough quality sleep, getting my health routine checks, and taking vacations to relax and recover. All these are progressing steps I practice daily toward a better, healthier lifestyle.

LEARNING SKILLS AND TOOLS

My university business education played an important part, as I was able to learn the different business terminologies that I now use daily. I don't need to know every detail, but I must have a general understanding of what I need in my business. For instance, understanding business profit and cash flow are two different things. You can have a very profitable business, but poor management can result in cash flow problems. Cash flow is the lifeblood of any business; therefore, it's critical you pay good attention to it.

Your business survival rates will be short-lived unless you track the cash coming in and out of your business. Sometimes it's a good idea to hire an accountant to look at your business operations; a different set of eyes might see areas which need improvement, and they can make recommendations on how to turn straight again. If you don't reach out for help sooner, a small problem can escalate to a bigger problem. Often, people try to fix problems themselves, or are in denial, or are too proud to ask for help. These attitudes only create more pressure.

We should all have a good understanding of the difference between an asset and a liability, and how each can work in our favor to create our wealth. I was keen to only look at the types of assets that will return my money, which was why I chose the pathway of property investing. In terms of liability, debt is used by some successful people to grow their wealth, but it has to be used wisely. My evaluation of good assets is something that will generate income for me not just today but for the long term.

Through this journey, I have witnessed a shift in my knowledge to better understand the language of business. Having a small business, it was vital I acquire the knowledge and skills to better run it.

As I travel my Auala, I have to motivate myself to engage in lifelong learning, as I need to enhance my understanding of the world around me. Changes are happening so fast, if I don't keep up, it can pose some unwanted risks to my business. Therefore, it's all about creating and maintaining a positive attitude in different developments of ourselves, be it personal or professional.

Skills of Communication

Communication is another skill people often pay little attention to, but I have invested a lot in improving my communication because of its many benefits. Good communication improves family and professional relationships. For some people, knowing how to communicate gives them the confidence needed to cope with public speaking.

When I left the island, my English was not that great. I didn't feel confident with the level I was at, especially after being out of school for a while. I surrounded myself with English-speaking friends, and that small change made a big difference to my fluency in conversational English.

Still today, I continuously have conversations with people to polish my English and, of course, make new connections with other people. I love it when people correct my English, because to me that is still part of my road to continuous learning. With my passion and love of books, I know my learning will never stop.

Being able to handle difficult situations makes you feel more empowered. That is a nice space for anyone to be in.

In my residential property business, I am in regular communication with my mortgage broker and property managers. My instructions need to be very clear, especially when money is involved and quick decisions need to be made. If I don't have the ability to liaise with them, they may misinterpret the message, resulting in unwanted results.

Communication at home is just as critical. In a marriage, it's important for a couple to understand the difference between conversation and communication. We have a lot of conversations which are general talks about how our day went, but we don't have enough proper communication where we talk out real issues. Marriage is hard work, but it can become harder when we don't focus on the things that make it hard. We, as women, have needs—and if they are not being met, it creates a tension between us and our partners. So talk things out, especially hard subjects, to combat the buildup of stress and marital issues.

Often, it is very hard for us to leave work stuff at work. Bringing problems from work to home with us is very common in some households—mine included. Our children and partners need our full attention. By choosing to be great listeners, we can help them with some issues they are going through. I use this simple question to open the conversation with my husband:

How was your day today?

Sometimes that one question can bring out issues he's debating in his head. I let him talk, and I don't interrupt. Then I ask the next question:

Have you finished, or is there more still to come out?

This is a good way to bring out things rather than bottling them up. Listening and talking openly is an excellent two-way communication skill to equip yourself with, because it strengthens relationships.

We battle a constant influx of information, which not only distracts our attention, but eats into our time. We have to look at how we can utilize our energy to create stability and simplicity in our lives. For our relationships to survive and succeed, we need to give them more care and attention. It's the same with our homes—to have a successful household, it requires cleaning and maintenance.

We have to put a lot of effort into our relationships, otherwise things will decay and will be hard to fix. Whatever amount of effort we put in, we should expect the same amount back. I leave you with this question to ask yourself:

How much effort are you putting into the things that really matter to you?

Every day, we encounter conflicts. In solving these conflicts, most people struggle to find the right solution due to a lack of skills. I strongly believe that having poor communication skills is a result of the lack of effort in prioritizing tasks in order of importance. Is your effort placed where it is most needed? Prioritizing tasks assists us in understanding where we need to concentrate our effort and how much energy we should contribute. The skill of effective communication is very much needed to produce positive outcomes.

Furthermore, we must understand that communication is very essential in everyday life. Things get done when they are communicated properly.

I believe many women lack the skill of communication. Consequently, they are denied opportunities that could positively impact their developmental progress. It is our job to practice effective communication skills. Finding the right Auala depends on having good and effective communications skills. As Robert Trujillo once stated, "As long as there is communication, everything can be solved."

Skills of Decision-Making

I get stuck overanalyzing things and waiting for more information before I make decisions. Although some would argue it's best to arm yourself with information before you jump, which I partly agree with, there are some great opportunities I missed out on because I didn't act quickly enough.

I have learned that it is worth the risk to make quick decisions, accept whatever the results may be, and move forward to the next decision. I've learned this separates the doers from the wannabes.

Every day, we are faced with decision after decision. Women are often good decision-makers. We are role models to our children. If our children see us as strong, they will imitate us; if we are weak, they will copy that, too.

My job as a mother is to ensure I support my daughter and build her up to be a mentally strong, independent individual. I believe regular family time has a huge positive impact on children. It builds a strong bond with our children, which will be critical as they grow. If we are present with them, we pass on important values they will carry for the rest of their lives.

Leadership

I take a leadership role in organizing my household, my business, my family's finances, my daughter's schooling, pick-up times, meal planning, after-school activities, and so forth. I am a full-time working mum, and this is my choice.

I want to give my girl my time and be present with her. It's sad to hear of women who work long hours only to get home close to dinnertime, too tired to spend quality time with their families. Unfortunately, this is the way some of us have to do things to make ends meet.

I want to continue to be an effective leader for my family. I have a sense of purpose and responsibility to make good choices for the best interest of my family. Being a good leader is being able to show a series of good behaviors and put processes in place so other family members can learn from them. It is about sharing experiences so others can deal with opportunities and challenges. Sometimes we learn skills through observation, and if certain skills fit our personal situations and provide answers to our problems, we will more than likely implement them in our lives.

I am always looking for ways to streamline monotonous activities with my business. After talking to my accountant, she suggested investing in an accounting software. After some thoughts and recommendations, I chose Xero. Using Xero, has made some of my tiresome routines less stressful. I used to use spreadsheets, but Xero has shaved off a lot of wasted time. Also, having the ability to be able to work from anywhere was a bonus. I try to stay on top of my paperwork throughout the year so everything is up to date and ready for the accountant. I need to get a good picture of our position early so we can see what we need to do for the next year and where we need to improve.

We seek to improve different aspects of our lives. Our attitudes can accelerate our learning. The more I saw my progress, the more I felt my other aspirations and goals were within reach, as well. The only barrier that exists between me and those goals is the one I set up myself. By learning the skills of information gathering, you are better equipped with making difficult calls in pressing situations and tight time frames. The Auala to a desired outcome will always require actions, and the actions you take will improve your chances of achievement. While your journey will take some twists and turns, you should never lose focus.

TIME IS A PRECIOUS RESOURCE

The most precious resource any human being has is time. As I get older, I realize how finite this resource is to me. Time is power, so I can be firm with my decision of how I want to spend my time. I don't just give away my time, because I know what little time I have is borrowed. I have to make sure I make the most of it.

The results from a study on how people use their time showed there were thirty-seven free hours per week. There is so much demand for our time, especially for women. We are superb at making ourselves available for everyone else but forgetting to spend time on the most important person: ourselves.

I believe the best use of my time is doing good work, having quality time with my family, having meaningful relationships, and looking after my own spiritual being. I am grateful God has blessed my life with abundance, and it is my purpose to share that abundance with others.

After my sister, Maria, had a breast cancer operation in late 2016 in New Zealand, she had radiation treatment until February 2017, after which she was clear to go home to Samoa. She was thrilled she was going home again, but things took another turn. The cancer came back, and this time it was very aggressive.

There was nothing they could do. It was heart-wrenching to talk about it, but my sister was very strong emotionally and spiritually. She knew her time was limited and was ready for what was in front of her.

I was tasked with giving her the news that her cancer was terminal. I didn't say it bluntly to her, and I regret not being as honest and direct with her as I should have. I learned to always be honest with conversations, even if it will be hard, because tough conversations create better learning and understanding.

We have to make sure we have good open communication and seek help early, so problems and concerns are dealt with. If we leave it until too late, time passes by and small problems grow into overwhelming burdens that affect our health and well-being.

I started looking closely at the time after the sad event of my sister's passing in October 2017. My brothers and sisters were very fortunate that we had a good week or so of quality time with our sister. We reminisced about the good old days, and she talked about how she wanted us to stay connected and be in peace with each other and with other people outside our family.

We should always make time to live life and share memories with the living. We were fortunate as a family that we got to say our goodbyes before she passed on, as other families never get that opportunity.

Always spend quality time with your living loved ones and treasure each moment, as they will not last forever in this lifetime. Our greatest asset is time, because we can do a lot with time when it is used wisely. Time spent with family heals us; time spent helping others fulfills our purpose and rejuvenates us. Time is precious, and we should never take it for granted.

There is no better time than now. I hear this almost every day in our everyday conversations. But yet we often fail to really absorb its trueness. With our own Auala, we experience bumps and smooth patches. I believe these things are there to test us, such as when I went through the events I've mentioned in this chapter with my sister's illness. It struck me in many different ways, and the lessons that came out of it spoke volumes. Life is precious. Some of the beauty of her life, as per my perspective, was her time with her family. In my eyes, she was lucky she got to see her grandkids. As for me, I still have that journey ahead, but what I know for sure is the best time ever is now to live and be present in the lives of the people who depend on me. That expression still rings true; we are here one moment, and then we are gone the next. Therefore, we shouldn't be spending time worrying and having negative emotions, because we will never realize the precious gift we have been given. Let's step into our best selves and ride out our journey here right now.

If you are still reading up to this part, I applaud you for following through my story. Let me reiterate that you have the attitude to make your dreams a reality, and by equipping yourself with the right unique skills, you can alter your pathway to get to the life you want to have. I am still walking my Auala, and I can vouch for what I have learned through my journey. I have overcome some of the challenges myself because of the self-belief that I could do it.

There are times in our lives we feel we are either growing or falling, but the important thing for us is to always remember our Auala (road traveled/pathway) to expansion becomes easier when we accept ourselves, accept our strengths, accept our weaknesses, and are open to what others can bring to our lives and fill up those potholes. Let me take you further to the next part of the journey to the second A of Auala, personal achievement.

"A" Represents Personal Achievement, and Why Does it Matter?

Why achievement was important to me then and now.

A—Achievement: We all aspire to achieve our own personal goals in life. While some experience academic achievement, other non-academics are still propelled through life and succeed in their own rights. I love reading about some amazing people who had little exposure to schools, then decided to drop out, and yet they still do extremely well in their chosen field. I believe that because of our uniqueness, we are also unique in our own way of learning. One size does not fit all, just like that common saying we hear all the time. Fit for purpose. The more I read about those individuals and their stories, the more I get motivated to keep charging ahead with my own fit-for-purpose learning to achieve my goals in life.

MASTER MY TIME

When my daughter was eight months old, I made a choice to put her through daycare so I could go back to work. It is difficult for a first-time mother to part from her child when he/she is still so little, but I didn't have my parents around for support. The only favorable option was to put her through daycare.

At the time, I felt a lot of guilt and nervousness, but reflecting back, I don't regret making the decision I made. I had to do what I had to do. We had bills and mortgages to pay, no different from other parents who also had young kids there.

I have incorporated yearly scheduled holidays into my family life. Don't wait until your financial position is in order before you take a holiday. My husband can't just get up and go for a holiday; he has to schedule his time wisely with his customers. It is not just about finding the time—it is about making the time. Usually his customers have been happy because they have been informed of his absence ahead of time. You have to make time. Saying you "don't have the time" is no excuse. You need to do a time re-evaluation, which might mean you have to make some serious commitments or tradeoffs in some other areas of your life. It comes down to what really matters to you.

You have to be an empowered woman to transform your life to the one which you've always wanted. With time mastery, whatever your goal is can be achieved. You have to be resourceful and courageous to achieve self-mastery, but it will become a bit easier with routines and proper time allocation.

I will never know how much time I have here on Earth, but every day I wake up, I praise God. I pray that he will bless me with more years so I can be around my daughter, to see what her chosen pathway will be and to witness the life she will lead.

We are living in a fast world with so many changes and distractions occupying our finite time. This requires us to be master of our own time. We, as women, have to be resourceful and good planners. Fortunately, I have been able to achieve things I set out to achieve because of my hungry attitude. It's like if you really want to have that best curry and you know a restaurant that makes superb curry is at the other side of town, you will drive to it even though you pass other restaurants along the way that also serve the same type of food. This is the same with our choices we make—if we want something so bad we will move mountains, we will find ways. It is only when we reach our intended goals we feel a sense of achievement, and it's there we feel we've put together one piece of the puzzle and can move to the next puzzle to solve—figuratively speaking, the next goal in life.

Focus and Pay Attention

I remember an embarrassing morning as I was heading out of the house to drop off my daughter, Hailey, and Miho (my international student from Japan) at school. My car came to a complete stop on the side of the road. I ran out of gas. I knew the petrol warning light had been on for about two days before, and I kept putting it off thinking I still had enough to get around.

I ran out of gas because I wasn't paying attention, but I also put so much on myself I couldn't put my attention where it was most needed. When we only say yes to our family members and coworkers, we are not prioritizing ourselves. We often try to prove to them we can perform everything, but any moment we can become overwhelmed and "run out of gas."

Turn your blinkers on. Make sure you have the right lenses as well, so you can clearly see the road ahead of you. Perhaps you will be able to anticipate things that come your way. We sometimes forget to pay attention to what is right in front of us because we are so busy rushing to get somewhere else.

This story reminds me to stop for a minute, take a step back, and be mindful of my own surroundings. We often focus on things that are not useful to us and then lose sight of the very important things. To maintain focus when I have a lot going on, I use a to-do list. I prefer to write things down, because I forget some things otherwise. I have also learned to say no when I need to, especially when I am faced with a dilemma. Learn to plan your day and work on the important things first. If you only do one thing on your to-do list, it's still a productive day.

I have been able to stay on top of most things on my to-do list because I have written it down. Although writing down tasks is good, if you don't make them happen and tick off the actions, you are not doing yourself a favor. It shows you are not paying attention and focusing on the important tasks you need to do. This relates to the previous chapter of being the master of your time. If you are not ticking those tasks off, my guess is your time is being consumed by other things. I have been there and still do, at times, struggle with focusing on what must be done. When I start thinking about why some actions need to be done, that action on my list all of sudden becomes super important when it really shouldn't be.

We all have different milestones in life we want to achieve, but it is up to us to be very objective with our thinking. This is where proper planning comes into the picture. For example, whenever we plan a family holiday, we go into this detailed planning mode of where we want to go, what we need, how long, clothes to wear, and so forth. We are good planners when it comes to that, and we go and enjoy ourselves and come back and tell our family of the experience. Well, that is an achievement. If we put that excitement of the planning of our holiday into other things we want to achieve for ourselves, just imagine the kind of lives we could live.

JOURNEY THROUGH REAL ESTATE INVESTING

One of the three goals I had prior to arriving in New Zealand was owning my own house. I felt a home would give me a sense of stability, safety, and security.

I didn't accomplish the dream of home ownership overnight. I didn't particularly know how it was going to happen, but I knew it would happen. God works in mysterious ways, like through my meeting with the bank about property investing. I only had $10,000 in the bank and didn't think that amount of money would buy a house, but soon I got a pre-approved loan of $155,000. I was ecstatic to know that from that small capital I saved, I was able to get a loan up to that amount.

Property investing was never in my family's blood. It was pretty much all up to me to find answers. My knowledge level was very limited, but my attitude was limitless.

My mind was wide open to absorb knowledge through books and other property investors. That early stage was more about the who and how questions. Who would help me accomplish this goal, and how can I set myself up to achieve success?

Jim Rohn once said, "For things to change, you have to change." I have always loved this phrase. It is for anyone who feels there is no progress in her life.

At first, I viewed real estate investing as a male-dominant playing field. So I was a little hesitant. How can I make it there? How can I put my stamp there? But now, being in that arena myself and experiencing it, I can honestly say it was my mindset that put those fearful thoughts in my head. I put myself there because I was listening to the external noises around me. Luckily, those noises didn't suppress me long. I achieved home ownership on my own, but if it hadn't been for my burning desire for this achievement, and seeking the help of others while walking my Auala, it would have been an impossible goal.

Possibilities

After my first real estate purchase, I started to take a lot more interest in property investing. I was hungry for information and eager to learn this new pathway of property investing. All the people I read about and heard in seminars kept saying, if you want to be rich and wealthy, you must invest in property. I had a lightbulb moment: Property investing is my new passion. Through investing, I can attain financial freedom and provide for those I love, as well as serving and contributing to other people's lives.

That thought was all it took for me to start my property investing journey.

Sometimes opportunities are not very visible to our eyes. And when there are situations that are apparent to us, we should always look behind those opportunities because of the possibility that there is much, much more behind it. That first initial real estate purchase opportunity opened my eyes to other possibilities, which led me to my new passion of property investing. I love this saying by Leslie Brown: "The only limits to the possibilities in your life tomorrow are the buts you use today."

We put many buts in some decisions we make; therefore, we lose some opportunities. We need to replace these buts and change our thinking from impossible to possible. Some of my personal achievements have not only helped with my development, but also led me to recognize some special moments of my journey with various people I have shared knowledge with, as well as making long-term connections and lasting friendships. The impact I had on their lives alone is a major achievement for me.

SELF-CONFIDENCE AND SELF-EFFICACY

It is very hard to stand in front of a group of people. People find public speaking so terrifying they rarely show up. They lack self-confidence.

My involvement in sports, beauty competitions, church gatherings, family reunions, and meeting different people from different walks of life all helped grow my self-confidence.

My greatest lesson for you is that you need to have lots of experiences in your life. Be adventurous, give things a go, do some traveling, visit a new place you've never been. You will be amazed at the experiment, trying different things, meeting different people. This will build your self-confidence.

When we take ourselves out of our comfort zone and step into unfamiliar territories, that is when we are really getting tested. It is those moments that define us. We make it to the next stage, or take our default position and stay in the safety zone. We either give up when things become hard, or have a breakthrough moment to follow it through.

It takes courage to try new things, to go on a different pathway. Concentrate your focus on what you can do, what works well, your skills, your talent, and everything good about yourself and your abilities. Believe in yourself.

Don't be scared to go up and talk to people. We too often wait for the other person to come and talk to us first, but the other person is thinking the same. If no one makes the first move, nothing will ever be shared, potential friendships will be lost, and business opportunities will be missed. So be bold and make things happen. The perfect time is now. You will be surprised at your capabilities and the new, self-confident person you will become.

Bidding in an Auction

Through my property investing journey, I only ever had two opportunities where I had to bid to buy two separate properties. I remember telling my husband I was just going to check it out and wouldn't bid.

I was very strategic in my thinking; I knew the potential buyer's purchase price, but I was not sure what the reserved price was and what the seller would accept. I also knew that this property had potential for subdivision, so my thinking cap was doing the hard work that night.

I waited until the end of the auction, then I approached

the agent who sold that property. I told her I wanted to be offered the opportunity to have a look at the deal if the last bidder decided not to go through with the purchase. Luckily for me, that man didn't go through with the deal, so they left it to me to decide whether to buy.

I understood the importance of not letting opportunities pass by when within reach. After some negotiations with the sales agent, I sealed the deal, and we were owners of the property that night. The very next day, my mortgage broker received a surprise phone call from me to complete the sale I just made the night before. He secured the funding, and we started working on our property development project.

We engaged the services of a good builder who we had formed a great relationship with over time. After a series of meetings with him and his team, we subdivided the section and built two brand-new townhouses.

I recommend to anyone planning a business venture to make sure you have a good team of people behind you. They should be the experts. Pay these people to do all those things you are not good at while you concentrate on what you are good at and what matters to you most.

When you gain confidence in yourself and your capabilities and start expanding your association with different people, you further develop yourself to learn new things and meet new people. You will notice the transformation in yourself.

Achievement is an important competency, I believe. As I reflect back on these wins, the more I have been able to follow through with my goals, the better my prospects were in achieving the things I wanted. My Auala has transitioned me to different lanes and pathways. Some were easy to get to, while some took a longer route.

It would be a lie if I said that I didn't have any interest in buying this property at the auction, even though I said to my husband I was just going to have a look. Of course, I had an interest. I had been talking to him about the potentials of it and even brought him along to view the property at the open house. So I had already envisioned what I was going to do with the property before the night of the auction. The things standing in my way were, if someone were to buy it for an unusually high price or I couldn't make it to the auction for some unseen reason. Thankfully, for me, everything worked out, and I came out a happy woman.

So achievement is something that you have done that is of significance to you; it may be at work, sports, passing your driving test, building a business, learning to play guitar, and so much more. It is those successes which have benefited yourself, your family, your company, or your community. Those are achievements because they are things we worked hard for, and at the end, our results speak for themselves.

As you can see, attitude permeates throughout these chapters. Knowing my true self and understanding what attitude is and what kind of attitude was required of me to show up in different areas of my life, I felt immensely empowered. Nevertheless, I had to be vulnerable and seek smart people who had the unique skills I needed to imitate, because it was those skills that moved those successful people to incredible heights in their success. Admittedly, it led me to really unclog the narrow thinking and limitations I had placed on myself, which led to some major personal achievements that I am very proud of and feel blessed to have been able to achieve.

Certainly, my Auala had all been little tiny steps, but the progression was nonetheless critical to my road to success. If none of those things were taking shape before my eyes, I would not have seen the possibilities. Reliability and timing kicked in as well. I had to rely on myself to push things ahead, because if I totally relied on others, the timing of the achievement of my goals would be pushed further away. This could lead to additional unwanted problems, such as a lack of motivation and self-doubt. For this reason, I believe when you want to lead your own life journey, you have to be your own leader. With this in mind, let me delve into the next component of the word Auala, L for leadership.

"L" REPRESENTS LEADERSHIP, AND WHY DOES IT MATTER?

L—Leadership: To begin with, I was always following the norm when it came to what was expected of me in my younger years. I guess this was because I was taught to obey and respect my parents and people with roles above me. Don't get me wrong, those are good values, but somewhere along the way, life throws you different challenges and scenarios that really stretch your thinking. Along with that, you meet different people, and you make your own observations and assumptions, resulting in you forming your own plan of action for your own career and personal aspirations.

That led me to becoming my own leader, leading my own way to my desired life. I had to be the one in charge of all the decisions I had to make, the decisions to leave American Samoa, my family, my support network, and all that was familiar and comfortable to seek a different life, all that I was longing for at that stage of my life. There are some challenges in Polynesian cultures, a prominent one being the ingrained role model of daughters being caregivers, while sons are encouraged to achieve. That is why I believe some women are trapped in those situations and are finding it hard to decipher their directions in life. So leaving that behind was all part of this Auala I had to take to my desired outcome. So the key thing here is we are all leaders in our own ways.

- ✠ **Mature mothers going back to school for more education; that is leadership.**

- ✠ **Moving to an unfamiliar country; that is leadership.**

- ✠ **Choosing which neighborhood to live in; that is leadership.**

- ✠ **Managing your money wisely so you are not living paycheck to paycheck; that is leadership.**

- ✠ **Sending your children to private schools; that is leadership.**

- ✠ **Speaking in conferences; that is leadership.**

- ✠ **Learning a new skill; that is leadership.**

- ✠ **Providing a home, security, and safety for your kids; that is leadership**.

- ✠ **Being able to manage people well; that is**

leadership.

The list can go on, but you can add this to your list of the actions you've taken yourself to move you to the next stage of your life. When I started listing down all the actions I had taken that led me to where I am today, I saw a different person. I really saw myself as a leader of my own life. Through writing them down and seeing them visually, it made me feel empowered. Those achievements, however small, showed strength, tenacity, and leadership.

This is a big deal because, when we finish this list, we see the results of our fire energy. Some women rely on men or other partners to take a leading role in all the decision-making. How then do you see yourself? What if something happens to that decision-maker in the house, and you are left with unwelcome surprises? Would you be ready to assume new roles and responsibilities?

Sometimes I hear of women who have had to start their lives again because of some problems in their relationships. This is still happening today. How would you feel? Keep asking yourself this question. I do it all the time, because it is not only for my purpose, but for my family. I want to know that if something happens, I know my family and I will be okay on various fronts.

DESIGN AND LIVE THE LIFE YOU WANT

What are you working on now? Do you know what legacy you want to leave behind? Everyone will have different answers, and some might not have any at all, but it is okay. Your whole life is about figuring that out. Life is a journey; it's about living and enjoying the process along the way. Sometimes we want to run before we walk.

I signed up for my first half marathon in Townsville, Australia, at the 1996 Oceania Athletics Championships, fifteen miles seemed overwhelming. I'd never run that distance, and I didn't quite know how I would do it. But I did it. I finished the race with my best time of 1:59:15, which resulted in a Bronze medal.

It was such a great satisfaction, knowing I have accomplished such an achievement. Although I was in competition with others, the real competition was against myself.

I could have easily not put my poor legs through the pain of pounding on fifteen miles of hard road, but the little inner voice kept telling me to go do it.

I had to keep pushing myself to not give up and to make it to the finish line. Back on the island, I had shin splint issues from running and playing netball on the hard surface of the courts. There were moments when my shins were feeling tight during the race, but I knew if I stopped, I might never forgive myself for giving up so soon. I thought of all the hard work I put into my preparation every day, the discipline, the sacrifices I had to make, the coach's time, and my family's support to get to that event and being able to compete on that day. That kept me going, and it's nice to look back and revisit those little wins.

I look at myself then and compare to today, and I think those characteristics still play a very important part in my life. I definitely had determination and the right attitude to make it to the finish line. All the pain disappeared the minute I passed the finish line. I love this quote by the late Zig Ziglar:

"Your attitude, not your aptitude, will determine your altitude."

I make a conscious decision to look after myself and have some alone time just to breathe and read a book. I even use my guitar to just play a nice tune and sing along to some relaxing songs. It is a good idea to always make sure I do things and have different experiences. I now make sure I set time aside to do traveling with my family. It's always nice to travel outside of New Zealand to explore other parts of the world and appreciate other places and their beautiful scenery.

Everyday, we are faced with so many decisions, it is important that we know and understand that we call our own shots. When I was young and living with my parents I had to abide by their rules. They were the decision makers for me then, but when I ventured out on my own, I quickly learned to be more independent and not solely reliant on them anymore. I challenged the status quo and I was okay with all that. My life is my responsibility and your life is your own too, so own it. You and I are unique and talented in our own special ways. It is our job to ensure we are doing all the things we love doing and experiencing the things we know would bring us massive joy and peace.

I volunteer at my Church through my service in the choir. Singing and worshiping God through music brings me so much joy. It's such a nice way to make new connections and get to know other people within our church community. It is a nice, calming environment to be in.

We were all born with different gifts. Some of us never realised our greatest gifts but some have propelled themselves to lead the lives they've designed.

The late Zig Ziglar once said:

"You are the only person on Earth who can use your ability."

He was a wise man. We should always remember, we

have choices. We can choose how we want to live our lives today, tomorrow, and the next day. We can choose who we hang out with, who we serve and who we impact.

I believe that we should always schedule some time to work and play. Life is short and we never know the time and day when it will get taken away from us. Make time to relax, play, and visit friends and family. No one will do it for you but yourself. This is you re-designing your life- -the life you are meant to have, not the one that someone else had designed for you.

By being true leaders, we are setting a foundation of our life plan--we are exhibiting traits that others can use and follow. Other true leaders before us, have paved the way and it's our obligation to keep it smooth for others to follow. It is also through my understanding of this invaluable skill of leadership, that I am turning this long-term dream of writing this book a reality. To tell my story so others who can see value and learnings and take charge of their own road to the different pathways to their success as I have with mine. My journey continues as long as I am still alive.

To Wrap Up AUALA

A—So I have enhanced my Attitude by being able to have control how I react and behave when faced with different challenges daily. My daily morning routine sets the tone of my day, and I try to maintain that throughout the day so I am always walking a straight path of my Auala

U—With my attitude, I have been able to hone in on Unique skills of communication and creating wealth so my family and I can live our lives with fulfillment, while also helping other family members.

A—My personal Achievements were within my reach because of my self-belief and self-motivation. I had a positive attitude about attaining them; I just needed to find the right people who could teach me the unique skills.

L—The essential skills of Leadership consist of being able to bring a positive attitude in all situations and being able to operate well under pressure. By keeping track of all my personal achievements and goals. I came to understand that I was a leader of my own Auala (road traveled). I took the initial step, and from then on, I kept accelerating myself to other levels and charged ahead to my desired outcome.

A—It was through this leadership role that I hope to inspire others to see that goals can be Accomplished. Our mindset needs to be strengthened and be flexible to play throw and catch. Filter out things that will get in the way of your accomplishments.

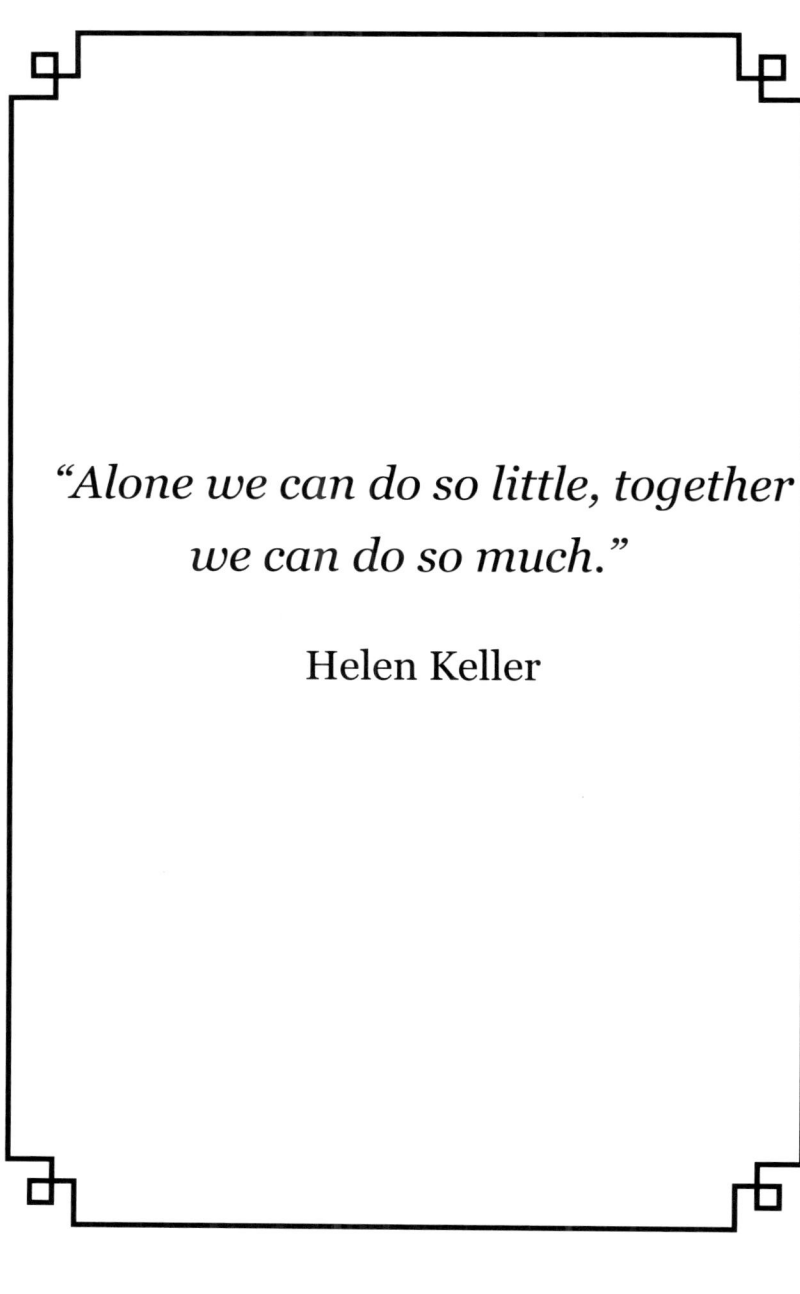

"Alone we can do so little, together we can do so much."

Helen Keller

HAPPY JOURNEY

It is my greatest pleasure to know that through this book I have contributed to someone else's life journey. It is a legacy I leave with my daughter, Hailey. Her journey might differ completely from mine, but the same principles will no doubt apply to her and her own family, as well as the many women she will connect to throughout her life.

I humbly hope as you read this book you feel inspired and empowered to stand tall and be courageous. Keep telling yourself that if she can do all that, then you can do it, too. If someone from a little island can come to New Zealand and achieve her goals to build a nice life here, then you can achieve the same success also.

Design your life how you want it. Devise small steps that, when done over time religiously, will get you to your perfect life with your family. You will be amazed with your results.

Perhaps you have some ideas in your head, but are still

hesitating before taking your next step. Stop thinking, and do it. Take that first step. The pain of regret is the last thing you want. Believe me.

Come join me. All it takes is having a great Attitude, combined with Unique skills, will result in personal Achievement, leading you to a different role of Leadership and helping with the Accomplishment of others, so that your life is your own blueprint and that has always been there for you to fully discover and live it.

Big shout out to all you empowered women out there in all walks of life for making those dreams a reality. I leave you with my favorite quote from one of the many mentors I routinely watch and listen to, Mr. Leslie Brown: "Other people's opinions is not your reality," and "You have greatness in You." Find your AUALA, and let us help others create meaningful lives.

ACKNOWLEDGEMENTS

I thank God for His blessings, which He has showered upon me, because without Him, I would not have been able to see this project through.

His blessings are the people who have brought me LIFE nurtured and supported me through my journey here on earth.

My loving parents, who are my guardian angels and who continue to watch over me. My sister who rests in peace for the inspiration to publish this book. The rest of my siblings for their support in many ways when I needed help. My mother-in law, my right-hand supporter at many times, and last but not least, my husband and daughter for giving me the time to focus on finishing my first book. The sacrifices have all been worth it.

A big THANK YOU to you all from the bottom of my heart.

REVIEW REQUEST

Thank you for choosing to purchase the book and reading my story, the navigation through the pathway to the life I now live.

I hope it has inspired you to take some necessary actions in order to transform your life, the one you are destined to have.

If you feel this book speaks to you and has helped you in any way, then please reach out to others and share with them how the book can help them too.

I would feel grateful and appreciative of your honest feedback and support as I continue this life long journey of empowering every woman I cross paths with every day.

Please take a few moments to leave a Review on Amazon.

Thank you ~ Sieni

To connect with me:

Email: –
auala.womenempower@gmail.com